Britain's Dreaming

for Melanie and Emma

BRITAIN'S DREAMING

Gareth Calway

Frontier Publishing
Kirstead, Norfolk NR15 1EG

First edition published 1998

ISBN: 1872914 24 1

British Library Cataloguing in Publishing Data
A catalogue record of this book is available from the British Library

Acknowledgements:

Part of *No Roman Stones In 1997* was first published in HQ Poetry
Quarterly.

Hallelujah Lampost sequence first published in Anglo Welsh Review.

Torfaen Monologues sequence first published in New Welsh Review.

The sestet of *Blasted* first published in Bare Bones.

Marked For Life first published in Footnotes and The Write Approach.

Norfolk Seen From The Welsh Mountains and *The North Sea* first
published in Poet's England 16: Norfolk.

Coalminer first published in Loose Change.

Angel first broadcast on Channel 4. (Hindi Picture)

Frontier Publishing and Gareth Calway gratefully acknowledge the help
and encouragement of King of Hearts Publications, publishers of
Coming Home by Gareth Calway

Illustration L.Aylmer
Typeset in Rotis Serif and Rotis Sans by
T&O Graphics, Bungay, Suffolk

Published with the Financial Support
of Eastern Arts and The Arts Council of Wales

Printed in Great Britain
by Crowes of Norwich

CONTENTS

to Claire and Tony

I

Britain's Dreaming

This year's girl describes you today
On my board in a balanced, feminine way

As "Unbalanced, unfeminine,
A pungent scorch on fine white linen,"

A pretty vacant judgement and proof
That there's never an easy time for truth...

This is a comprehensive selection from Boudicca; Britain's Dreaming, a masked poetry show performed by Never Mind The Testsosterone, Here Comes Boudicca Company.

It tells the story of Boudicca's revolt against Rome and patriarchy in the First Century A.D. ("I'm no Elsie/ I'm the flint-white pearl/ The finest hour/ Of the Norfolk girl!") It also tells of the bard's enduring love of her as matriarch and Muse.

Boudicca (Boadicea) was Queen of the Iceni (Norfolk and Suffolk) until the death of her husband Prasutagus in 60 AD. Recognising only kings, the Romans seized her territory, looted and enslaved her people, raped her daughters, flogged her when she protested and generally set about imposing the patriarchy which would become Roman "civilisation". The tribes of Eastern Britain, seething under twenty years of similar oppressions and insults, now rose in revolt beneath her, leaving first Roman Colchester, then London and St Alban's burning in their wake. When the professional soldiers of the Ninth Legion marched out from Lincoln in the early days of the revolt to arrest her, Boudicca's Britons annihilated them as well. She put her soul-foe, the money-grubbing anally retentive treasurer Decianus Catus ("The old dicky anus deputy head"), to humiliating flight. Her passion and fury met its match, alas, in the cold military logic of Governor Suetonius Paulinus in AD 61, just when it seemed she would drive the invaders back into the sea they came from 20 years earlier. To avoid capture, she took poison. Though the long term effect of her revolt was to make the Romans more temperate in their treatment of their subjects, the punishments they meted out to the revolt's perceived ringleaders – the Iceni – were so brutal that the Earth-held evidence of last ditch resistance, salted fields and retarded remains still tell a story carefully omitted from the accounts of Roman historians (from which nineteen hundred years of subsequent accounts have been drawn.)

The punk rock mood of No Freedom, No Future, No Fun – of hippy ideals balked, exhausted and finally kicked over in favour of something more desperate ("The Summer of Love burning out into one blistering Night of Lust, into Nothing") – is evoked as a paradigm of these First Century Celts, their eco-culture dispirited, their Earth Mothers destroyed by money-straights, their subsequent all-or-nothing-Eros-against-Death revolt burning out all too quickly in a brilliant blistering flame – into nothing. The account of Boudicca's final battle (with its catastrophic defeat of Britain's Dreaming) is referred to in the show as The Clash.

I Britain's Dreaming

Crowded House are singing
"Julius Caesar
and the Roman Empire
couldn't conquer
the blue sky"
and I think of you, Boudicca,
with that same sense
of singing triumph
even though your glory days
were under grey skies
and short-lived
and weren't innocent
or cornflower-pretty
as some Celtic blue summer
and had more to do
with this Norfolk flint
and stubborn soil
than an air of heaven
and even though
Suetonius Paulinus
and the Roman Empire
seized the sunrise
of your three easy wins
as if seizing the flames
of your famous red hair,
and even though
Suetonius Paulinus
and the Roman Empire
crushed your country
if not your body
in his square Roman fist
sowed harvests of hunger
rubbed decades of salt
in your people's wounds

the old word
buddug
still sings in my Welsh blood,
in the Norfolk winds
off this unresting sea

buddug:
buddig[1]:
victory

1 An ancient British word surviving in the modern Welsh *buddugoliaeth*

II Anarchy

I want to sing about Boudicca because
I love her woad-caked brythonic majesty.
(Strict stuffy Latin master Julius Caesar
Named the Britons thus: Pretanni: Painted folk,
While Boudicca played truant in the art room
With blue clays and her bra off. Who
Would you rather spend the afternoon with?)
I love her fecundity, (The fact
That she wouldn't hide the power
Of earth-words in a Latin fudge like "fecundity").
I love her ferocity. Hell had no fury
Like a matriarch scorned and three
Roman colonies caught it, the barracks
Of those ramrod rapists burning down
Over their heads, a riot of hooves
IN THE CITIES OF THE DEAD... – I love that
Because it's what ought to happen
When <u>any</u> mother's back is flogged by a prick
Like Decianus Catus, any mother's daughter
Plucked and plundered: She ought to be a revenge
Archetype, a maternity myth:
Perhaps she was once. Now she doesn't fit.
She's the round Earth goddess the Romans buried
Under straight roads and patriarchal order,
The fascist composure of the fasces, the drilled
Decimation², the retarded skeletons
In Iceni burial grounds...
She lacked these civilised virtues.
But I still feel the hysteria rising
In her veins, the menstrual flow that crashed
Like the North sea, that stormed her victory
Against the ironskirts, still feel it freeze,
Her chief bard wince, as they flayed her back,
Forced garrison lust on her daughters
Still see that bloody mane came up
In dark knowledge, *"They shouldn't have done that"*
Then fly for the throat – like a wild voodoo warsong
Strung on a bard's harp -
And tear it to shreds. Right
Now ....
Ha ha ha ha ha... I love
The fact that she went all the way.

² this word originated in the Roman practice of cutting enemies into ten equal pieces

III   Safe European Home

My Muse has been very patient with me,
Waiting demurely for me to turn to her
From dramas of Romano-British women,
Grammar School Muses
(Muses with quads and Latin mottoes)
Vivianes and Guineveres,
Made up women whose woad comes from Paris,
Whose god-lover *Llugh* translates himself
As "Lancelot Du Lac", (Lancelot of the Lake)
Whose scent isn't animal
Just tested on animals; whose fabulous
Scarlet and sapphire long silk dresses
Are the art that conceals art, the romance
That conceals sex. So naked Boudicca
Turns at last, shakes out her fiery locks,
Lifts me up by my bardic lapels, and says
I am your Muse, and forces her furious lips on mine
And believe me
With that tongue in my throat, that heart in my mouth
Beating out Boudicca, boudicca, boudicca
I want to sing her dark voodoo warsong
Like it's never been sung before.

Boudicca boudicca boudicca

I want to ride that chariot with you

Boudicca boudicca boudicca
in my heart beat
boudicca boudicca boudicca
in my pulse pump
boudicca boudicca boudicca
in my heart punch
boudicca boudicca boudicca
in my pulse thump
boudicca
in my blood heat
boudicca
in my heart jump

boudicca
in my horse feet
boudicca

death-black, *wide-eyes, blood-red dyed hair blown back*
horse-brassed ball-smack whip-crack kick-back
bold boudicca
let the bared breasts ride tonight
cut a chariot dash with a woad-caked arse
lash a sea wind to your thighs

bad boudicca...

boudicca boudicca boudicca

boudicca boudicca

boudicca

boud
i
ca

a

I'm kissing the faceless dead ground
On the breast of a Norfolk rise,
Embracing the chill winter grass
With all my body, with all my heart,
And into my mind steps a beautiful maiden
The spirit of some lost Celtic summer
Touching my skin.
Imagine a rowan, her May leaves wet,
Kissing your shoulder with late spring rain,
Imagine your mind like a moistened bud
Drinking her sweetness. Imagine her leaves
Turned light side up with the weight of her berries
August-heavy in the full milk moon.
Imagine her berries
Spilling their juices like healing oils
Over your November loneliness.
That's how Mother Boudicca loves you...

                    But what if she's
A death cup, brimming with poison? what

If this bare-armed Bronze Age queen
Is taking me where I've no stomach to go?
I shiver and rise from her poor dead arms
In my raw winter night, hearing soft weeping
Pass on a warm breeze, sense honeyed birdsong,
A deep bronzed arm,
                    my pale skin petalled
With flowers from a summer 2,000 years gone...

IV Boudicca Speaks

The incredible aliveness of trees,
The angel-brightness of stars (humming harmony)
The hammering breath of <u>being</u> here
Arms aloft in the holy grove
–Oak trees and rowan, hawthorn and misteltoe-,
Naked eyed under the naked stars.
Skinned to the night breeze, naked-weaponed.
I am nothing but bark and leaves.
Stretching myself to the cloud-stripped sky,
Stretching my skin in the horsetongue grass.
Undressed to kill.

I hear the ageless druid music
Much nearer the surface – the soilskin – that you'd think
(Pockets of wild amid Rome's cultivation)
IN THE CITY THERE'S A THOUSAND MEN IN UNIFORMS
I shiver with the gnosis of being.

(Rome has foisted deals on us all our lives
In return for not conquering us.
Compromised futures, compromised freedoms, compromised
fun.)

I want to run forever through this dark grove
Slimy underfoot with November leaves
Breathe deeper than the sea which rolls
Five miles away in the caverns of my ear

I want to drown my days
In this infinite Breath of being,
Reality behind the insanity.
I'm tired of wearing habits,
the colours of my tribe,
my drag-queen's drab,

I am baring my soul for battle.
I've been angry for years.
I've been fucking angry.
I'm not going to put up with having Romans on top of me
anymore.
THERE'S NO CONTROL OVER WHAT YOU WANT AND
THERE'S NO CONTROL OVER WHAT YOU NEED

Don't know what I want but I know how to get it.

And if it doesn't work atleastyoucansaywetried.

V London's Burning

In The City...

The orgy was under way.
We'd gone down an absolute storm at Camolodunum
They were calling it Dun Camulus – the old British name – in
our honour.
The sweet smell of screaming, bloody rucking suck-sex,
That kick-to-the-balls annunciation, that world-shattering
Anarchy tour:
Never mind the Romans:
Here Comes Boudicca and the Banshees,
Here Come the Stranglers. Here Come the Damned.
To town near you. Now.
And what a town!
Proto-Essex Man Colchester!
The model Roman Urb, the colony Camolodunum,
The sound of the suburbs
Rocked to its foundations, show homes stomped to a cinder,
Whooshed in the fire that flamed from my loins.
And there were some neat little gigs to come: The Big One at
the St Alban's Empire -Verulamium
Some out-of-town fortresses to raise the roofs at,
Knocking the Ninth Legion dead near Lincoln,
Giving them head in true Celtic fashion
Heads and dugs will rock and roll; all of them except
That plodding heavy metal joke they call a cavalry – the alae–
Who scarpered.

Now we're on the road again – the Roman road, straight as a
sword -
To little old Londinos on the Father of Rivers,
Londinos, the Britain the Britons have lost
In vitae imperium
Nil futurus Nil liberatus tedius librium Londinium.
Never Mind the Pansy's People and Pseudo-Greeko dreaming
Disguising the Roman bankers and the new-rich salemen
scheming,
Never mind the fat cats in their new-rich concrete flats,
Never mind the Roman tick-accountants and marts,

Never mind the admin blocks with iron-skirted guards,
Never mind the humdrumming Boredom Now,
Here Comes The Pogo with Death and Co.
Here Comes Blood Spitting Anger Joe.
HERE COMES BOUDICCA!

London's Burning!
LONDON'S BURNING!!!!!

Babylon's burning.

VI God Save The Queen

I am history, not myth, but remember
History is written by the victor
And I neither wrote nor won
No freedom, no future, no fun.

Rome had to win or lose the Empire,
Britain had to win or simply expire,
And with it the Western horizon,
No freedom, no future, no fun.

Procurator Decianus Catus
Spoke down his nose, spoke down his anus,
"The Emperor claims the dead king's kingdom."
No freedom, no future, no fun.

"Our Roman matrons have their place too
In a civilised home: I could offer you
A place in mine: dresses, <u>baths,</u> decorum."
No freedom, no future, no fun.

I danced to the wardrums, warhooves, hornwhine,
Exhorting, as Romans were drilled into line,
My race to fling back the squares of London
No freedom, no future, no fun.

Now my rebels hole up, where home is none,
On roots thin as hope and a dream of Britain,
Hunted through thickets and twigs, their soles stung:
No freedom, no future, no fun.

My hard core Iceni's last stand and fall
Is the longest, fiercest, stubbornest of all
But is crushed – like flint – in the Battle at Thornham.
No freedom, no future, no fun.

Death-and-glory queens, country dragons:
(Become) Whores of fashion in Camolodunum,
In Roman roses our own scent gone.
No freedom, no future, no fun.

My salts that I sowed in the Squareheads' wounds
Return in a wash that will sour our lands.
I loosen my tongue on its poison:
No fun, no future, no freedom.

VII Choral Ode Of Iceni Ghosts/ Norfolk Nature Sprites

Strophe

We're the restless ghosts in the winds and rains,
Funneling the valleys, sweeping the plains,
Inlets and warrens that run underground,
Unbridled pathways, unquiet streams,
Haunted hidden corners of rootless sound,
Hives of Iceni, dead and unqueened,
By bronzebreasted redcrests violently weaned,
We're the baby who wails for her dead mother's breast.

Antistrophe

We are dead keening women, whispering grass,
The breath in the lilac and bluebells, the blast
Through the pale yellow oak leaves, hawthorns
And nettles. And that shout, queen of warriors,
From your victory chariot with your triumphant
Horsemen around you! And that salt chill of a winter's
Reprisals that blighted twice twenty summers.
We're the mother who wails for her new baby's death.

Epode

We are the cries in the corn, the harrowings hooted
Under moons of hunger, in the squeals of the hunted,
The creaking of geese through night-forest fears,
The unresting dunes and the moaning wave-break,
We're the memory that's cankered two thousand years
Of Celtic blood with an unhealing ache,
We're the oracles lost in the noise diggers make.
We're the dead daughters wailing for the end of the world.

VIII No Roman Stones In 1997

("school...where they teach you how to be thick")

The Romans with their straight conquering lines, expressive of the will. The principle of getting from Alpha to Omega by the straightest route possible.

and the Celts with their curves based on the woman's body, the generous breast, the long lazy voluptuous hip, the ocean swell of the pregnant belly

The Romans, pedestrian.
the Celts equestrian

Why has it taken history so long to give you your right name, Voada, Voadicia, Bonduica, Bonduca, Boadicia, Bunduca, Bunduica, Boadicea?

The ancient Celts called you *buddig* – victory.
Modern Celts – on the rare occasions they get a victory-
still call it *buddugoliaeth*
(The nearest modern Norfolk gets is, boodiful.)

Why has it taken art so long *not* to give you a painting or a sculpture
That isn't basically neoclassical,
Basically a Roman view?

It's either a Vestal Virgin cameo as Mater Brittani*cas*
or great bonking barbarian breasts and a barmy army.

Why have the poets and dramatists always given you a subordinate role in your own drama?
outside odds on your own course?

Why has that Roman concrete lasted so long?

Why has it taken Western culture nineteen hundred years to wonder whether we backed the right horse?

We cannot act for you, great mother,
We are the future dreaming of your holly-shafted chariot
Sprung on the wind.

I go to a teacher trainers' conference in Cambridge.
The collective noun for Norfolk trainers is Iceni.
The conference leader is Unreconstructed Cambridge man:
silver arm bands, silver eyebrows, gold cufflinks, bronze tie pin.
A Celt cavalier in a Roman age.

Wild geese flying over the playground today: the first time
I've ever noticed them at work.
The Iceni reared them as semi-sacred pets.
I write:
These almost holy geese swimming the winter sky
The Romans would just cook them and eat them in a pie.

The Head of Psych. tells me that all poets are a bit mad.
It must be what I have in common with you, Boudicca,
Moon-horses loose in the top pasture.

Why am I talking to you, *Mam Gymraeg,*

– on your horse-people's chalk and flint plains,
   on this soil of a glacial frontier,
   by this free wild thing of light and water
   (here where you lived and rode and died)

Why am I talking to you, mother of Britain,

– in this time of the nerd and the trainspotter,
   in this time of Little England without Britain,
   in this time of training without education
   (in this time of the Essex man)

Why am I taking to you, victory queen,

– waling among flint-toothed fields
   at the roots of a tongue that gets lost in translation,
   drinking dandelion and rowan in a ditch of roman nettles
   from a freshly exhumed celtic love cup,

I'm no matriarch's footling, after all this time,
   (a follower, though, in no mean measure
   of the wild track of your spirit,
   of your celtic war cry ringing long:
   one who would at least try to sing your song),

Why am I talking to you
Like you're a problem parent in a school
Where the school is the problem...?

Because no-one else understands a word I say.
Because, although like you I have kicked
Against the tight-arsed pricks of this world
And lost, unlike you I have the power to record
That defeat in sentences. Because although
The spirit of AD 60 is still in Janus's office
For wearing fishnests and leather

And writing *Bollocks* in the girls' toilets
Signed *Vicky Briton,* I'm still outside,
Free this period and everywhere in chains,
Because she's making a stand, embracing
Her bondage, legs easily apart, heart unbridled
Beneath the tight bra. Because her look
Is your bladed blood-haired mask with a tragic
Woad-striped barbarian face. Because
She is Delacroix's *Liberty* thirty years after
The Last Page of History: that dread-wrenched
Look of Auschwitz Prisoner 1507 sniffing
"Arbeit Macht Frei",[3] *"Lasciate Ogni
Spernaza Voi Ch'entrate"*[4]
– "No Freedom No Future No Fun" –
In the poison fartgas of the most terrifying
Anally retentive control freaks of all time.
Because she is
Prickly, mistress-heeled, punky,
Zipped, studded, safety-pinned, padlocked,
Eye-lashed, brow-razed, crowfoot-painted,
Animal/ sharp/ spiky/ spunky/
Everywhere in chains. Free

                       Ah! because
She's the spit of you in your buzzing prime,
A "naked woman with strong breasts",[5]
Striding over barricades
With sturdy male warriors behind her.
Because she's the daughters you never really had,
The heirs of Britain who didn't inherit,
The street-princess who doesn't want to be
A trainee all her life in some patriarch's
Empire. Because she's the Summer of Love
On amyl nitrate, one blistering Night of Lust
Burning out into two decades of anal reaction
*(Shock-haired philistines in power suits,
The hateful straights of the eighties.)* Because
She's ballsy, out of control, unhappy...

                    Because no-one
Understands *her* either.

[3] Work makes free: the greeting inscribed on the gates of Auschwitz
[4] Abandon all hope ye who enter here: the message inscribed on the gates of Dante's Inferno.
[5] Delacroix's definition of Liberty.

IX What's So Funny ('Bout Peace, Love and Understanding)?

Spring has come to Norfolk at last
On Siberian winds and rain
Keeping our holiday home neighbours
Safely in Colchester.
Five miles inland I can smell the sea,
Taste the salt on the wind through the green corn.
Mares are getting frisky, flirting their manes
At stallions in the meadows. I fed them at dawn
With my daughter, their flanks hot with freedom.
Workmen curse ancient foundations in concrete
Under the yard of our flint cottage;
I don't think they hear the ghosts
I hear as I empty ash from the aga;
It's not a good idea to do it in a hurricane.
The ash whips round, *lashing the air*
Like a cry of pain and rage and goes flying
Into my eyes.

Ashes blowing on a summer wind
From a winter fire that burned all too bright
And all too briefly two thousand years ago.
Your ashes. Bold, beautiful, Boudicca.

There was pollen spent in bogland then
Settling on dead Iceni lips
Blown on the winds of their fleeing
Which survives intact even now...
The only thing that breaks its skin
Is its female counterpart.
The Romans were that unfertilised
Pollenskin, outlasting you, Boudicca,
Frigid as columns of concrete,
Fearing that fatal contact. My words are
A storm of bachelor pollen, they seek you,
It only needs one of them to reach you...

It only needs a moment.
A moment like yours:

When the columns of Gloria Mundi,
The pillars of world power,
Were seriously shaken
And the course of history faltered,
May even have been altered.
A moment when the woman
Gave way to the man
But not without a fight.
A moment, as this dank May dies
Like the wind's Iceni gossip through the massed
Spears of corn and a June
Sun kisses the glades at last,
When I feel a real time beneath
Even this legendary robin-hood green,
– Even this Eighteenth Century
World-transforming
Scientific farmland -
A Bronze Age Forest
Within the yawning woods,
A beat in the undergrowth,
An air in the trees,
A heat that threatens to shatter
In thunder and end the very world
Flash-photoed by lightning...
Will I meet you at last here, now?

I wait all day and then come home
But at night it's the same.
I can't sleep. I go out,
Hot Bronze Age blood pulsing
In my areolae, my lawn
A jungle floor, the quaint
Get-away-from-it-all backwoods
Pre-motorcar Estate Agent ghost
The village pretends to be
Fading like a mist
Into the "pentref Celteid" it is.

With a moon in her prime,
A moon with a dark side
Breasting the blue,

A star-sparkling
Boat in a sea of blood,
A Boudicca moon.

And a woman's voice in the dark
Soft and heavy and strong.

And I realise. You don't ask if it's a death cup
Or lipped with honey. You drink it anyway.
That's what love is. *Surrender.*
The throat's submission to the song.

And I drink, deep and dark and long.

To Mum, Dad, Ruth and Donna

II

Mountain Ashes

In Wales, it was believed that the Mountain Ash had furnished the Holy Cross and for this reason it was widely planted in cemeteries. (It was believed to stop the dead from rising). *Encyclopaedia of World Mythology*

Rowan or Mountain Ash was greatly venerated by the Druids and was formerly known as the "witchen" because it was supposed to ward off evil... Many mountain-ash berries are said to denote a deficient harvest. *Brewer*

Ash: The powdery residue, chiefly earthy or mineral, left after the combustion of any substance... A symbol of grief or repentance. *O.E.D.*

Mountain Ash (Aberpennar). Industrial town, Cynon Valley district, mid-Glamorgan. Its growth dates almost entirely from c1850 with the exploitation of rich reserves of coal and only after about 1945 were factory industries significantly introduced to offset the serious fall in mining employment. *Encyclopaedia Brittanica*

I Got On At Hallelujah Lampost
Hallelujah Lampost is the name of a bus stop between Blaenafon and Varteg Hill, high up in the Eastern Valley of Gwent/ Monmouthshire. These excerpts are from a sequence describing a conductor's view of the bus route concerned in 1980, shortly before conductors were phased out altogether. The sequence was published in Anglo Welsh Review in 1985, by which time the coal industry had joined the steel industry at the back of the longest dole queue since the 1930s. Friends, I was that bus conductor.

Torfaen Monologues
Torfaen is a borough drained by the river Afon Lwyd, after whose attribute, *torfaen:* rock breaker, it is named.

The Heavy Metal Sonnets
Christopher Mills (Red Sharks Press) suggested the title. The sonnets tell the story of Valley Bryn meeting Newport Bron and subsequently of sex, drugs, heavy metal and lapsed nonconformism in the Bristol Channel port/ capital of Gwent. (The opening two sonnets of the full sequence may be read in New Welsh Review No.23. under the title Newport Nocturnes.)

Yellowing Lines
I was offered my first teaching job while in the basement bogs of the Cwmbran Development Corporation's multistorey carpark, the week before my driving lessons began. *Double decker bus* driving lessons, courtesy of my employers The National Welsh Omnibus Co. The inveterate eighteen year old hitch hiker in me chose to go back to the classwomb instead. A few years later, he'd changed his mind...

Marked For Life
No-one forgets a crap teacher. Nowadays, she'd be running a Linguistics department at the Gradgrind and Woodhead Back to Basics Institute offering Poetry By Numbers INSET to English teachers. Oh, yeah, and working for Ofsted.

Ofsted
Millions of pounds are being spent by successive Governments to "improve" Education. No, not to provide dry and temperate classrooms, books or equipment (apart from that glorified pen/calculator called a Computer) but to bring teachers into line with a bureaucrat's monster called The National Curriculum. This monster forces English teachers through so many contortions that another monster needs to be called in to extricate them from their own backsides every time they plug in a programme of study. *This* money-devouring monster is called an Ofsted Inspection. We had one at our school recently. Imagine Paris in the last few days before the Gestapo arrived and you'll get the atmosphere. Imagine Planet Earth invaded by Saturn and you'll get what actually happened.

The Road To Walsingham
This is about a trip out to Little Walsingham with some friends. Walsingham is a pilgrimage site because Richeldis de Faverches had visions of the Virgin Mary there in 1061. I didn't.

The North Sea.
When I first moved to Norfolk, this sea really felt a long way North, Arctic, out on a limb, a long way away from real blue southern seas like the Mediterranean or the Indian Ocean, a long way from where things were really happening. Then I went to India and felt exactly the same there too so I realised it was me. Now I feel utterly at home with the North Sea: the way the light is so variable over every inch, variable from minute to minute, like it never is further south, the glorious gull and geese-wild Northern greyness of it. What the author of Beowulf would describe as "the wintry whale road." In this poem I attempt to describe the majesty and rhythmic might of the North Sea by becoming it.

I Got On At Hallelujah Lampost

• 3. Fire & Brimstone

This valley had iron
In its guts,
Steeled itself to change,
Moving with the trains,
Dug into its coal
For a port for the ores of Spain.

It had shod the Great Bear
Of the Steppes with skates
Made In Blaenafon,
Had united the States
Across the wild west
With Monmouthshire iron.

And when King Coal called
For a Copper Grail
For his stainless steel Table,
Tongues of fire could purge
The iron in the soul
At Pontypool inferno.

• 4. Conductor

The conductor stubs out
Nostalgia and fag
For the rush down valley,
While through his worn bag
Go all the colours of the river,
The green and the silver and the discoloured copper,
Changing
Forever.

• 5. Afon Garde

     Afon raging with the rain.
The cut steelworks sinks in the sodden clay.
Steel-faced pickets slam a portcullis
And draw up the bridge of their riverbank scrapyard:

   The workers
   United
   Will never be defeated.

Red-soiled, livid, steaming, green,
Fed with liquid fire and gases,
Afon, desperate, blindly burrows
Like a dragon for the sea.

> And the Sunday School kids
> Are Monday-morning singing...
> *The Word*
> *Is on the dole*
> *He'd rather give us the past tense of coalfield.*
> *Emmanuel*
> *Is on the dole*
> *He's gone down the drain with all the rotten leaves.*

Panteg steelworks at twelve o'clock,
Busmen chasing overtime, pickets – jobs,
Eyes calm as anthracite,
Clouds lined with lead:

> *The workers*
> *United*
> *Will never be defeated.*

6. New Towns For Old

> In Tal-y-waun
The girls are like leather, the beauty ingrained,
In 15, at 50, it remains, on the wane,
Like the ghost of Coal always in the unworked vein
And what is already has, and what has will again
In Tal-y-waun.

> In the the New Town
> In the the New Town
> In the the New Town
> In the the New Town
The old canal is polished up, the gardens laid down,
And pushchair trolley women bus aroundaroundaround
And brakes and valves and services – autopias – abound.
Parked in his mother's arms high above the ground,
The brand new Son of Cymru gives a multistorey frown ,
MORE of lots of MORE to lose, mortuary-bound,
And after six, just trodden chips-
> Not a soul to be found.

Torfaen Monologues

1

Behind some old shed
Down by the river
I'm tugging at Sian Davies's bra fastener.

"See you again," she'd said,
Her eyes boring *I want you* into mine
So candidly even I believe it.

Now I'm tugging at Sian Davies's bra fastener
And wondering what I'm supposed to do next.

She could tell me. If I could ask her.
But I stopped being nakedly honest like that
Since it made me appear the only male virgin in the Year
group.

So I'm pretending it's never in doubt.
I listen to the river roaring by
And tug at Sian Davies's bra fastener.

2 decades later I'm a Head of Department
Still pretending I know what I'm doing.
I've been pretending that for twenty years.

What I'm really doing is hiding behind a shed
Down by the river Afon Lwyd
Tugging at Sian Davies's bra fastener.

2

The Boys
And me
 We're off
Up The Cooler.
 Climbing the wastelands
Brickwork ruins
 Slag mountains
Rusted rolling stock
 Summer woods
             Out above the treeline.

I'm tired. It's hot. I'm sunburnt and thirsty.
The Boys pick some berries I've never heard of.
They're all harder than me.
My arm aches from punches.

The Cooler. They keep going on about how great The Cooler is.
It turns out to be a rusted tank of water next to the pithead
                                    tasting of pit-dust and iron.
Some miners watch us sneaking in.
Their faces are black like bruises.
They look the other way, grinning to themselves.

I pretend to enjoy it,
Dive headfirst into a splashfight.

Tecker picks a scrap so I swing my fist at his temple,
Get blood on my knuckles,
Iron in my soul,
A baptism into coalfield manhood.
Scrap! Scrap! Scrap! Scrap! Scrap! Scrap!

     3
Getting off the bus after school.
Gritty steps.
A smell of diesel, tobacco and old-carpet seats.
Reminds me of my Old Man.

I wave up at a face in the clouded window. She smiles back
vaguely.
She was showing me her milky thighs all the way home.
I was sitting next to her.
I held on tightly to my bus ticket and didn't do anything
about it as usual.

I call in for the Old Girl's daily bread order.
I hold the loaf out in front of me like a Rugby ball,
Run sidestepping down the road as if scoring a try for Wales
Pretending that's what my fantasy is
So that people will like me.

No-one's watching.

God, I hate Rugby.

I hate Rugby.

     5
My Uncle Dai
Fists broken playing Rugby for the Town team
Gut swelled with endless pints of *Wind & Piss*.

Every Christmas, a treasure chest of chocs for my mother.

A packet of five cigars for Dad.

Dad doesn't smoke.

I'm fourteen and *nesh*.
I'm facing Uncle Dai at soccer
On the Bob-A-Day rugby pitch
(Levelled from the slag by the unemployed
In those *Never Again* 30s.)
I watch him coming at me.
He's built like a mountain of Pennant grit.

I tap the ball sideways, dance to one side
And leave him standing.

I can beat him.

I can beat the bastard.

      6
My Old Man
National Service tattooed arms
DEATH OR GLORY,
Face set like mine two decades on.

Redundant.

Three years ago they privatised his industry.
Two years ago they privatised his pension.
They've given him a testimonial.
It says he's indispensable.

We're driving the family to the coast in my car.
It feels funny to be doing it instead of him.

It's hot in Barri.
Chips with everything
Except fish.

All the way home the sun beats down.
Gothic ruins of docks, mines, steelworks.
Slagheaps half-mossed with heather.
Fibreglass windscreens and motorshowroom windows
      dazzling my eye as they catch the sun.

My Old Man
Anger buried under the shock in his face,
Staring through the windscreen

Not seeing much.   1991

The Heavy Metal Sonnets
Valley Bryn and Newport Bron

"In the days of my youth I was told what it means to be a man.
Now I've reached that age I try to do all those things the best I can.
But no matter how I try I find my way to the same old jam..."   *Led Zeppelin*

2 Chemotherapy (Bryn)

My folks wrote me off. The racing, strangetown bus
Was less a wreck that day than me. I lodge
With Dr Junkhi in a bedsit-and-bodge.
He's – catcrap stiffens his old hippy rugs-
Just Divorced. My sheets itch with cold and bugs.
My taste for abrosia's petrified to stodge:
Tranquil lies with Barb and Mand, randy splodge
Of Nursey flesh: I live on capsules, slugs.

Doc. writes scripts for speedy cures for some girl
Who like his paranoias *may* exist.
He saws through wires and floors to fox The State.
His mind, starved of Morphine, is a whirl
Of plot and counter. Mine's a stony cyst
Of fear. Neither cures my sleepless self-hate.

3. Unholy Family (Bron)

So your ma's kicked you out? you're on the street
A term before you sit your first exam:
That narrowminded sheephead you call "Mam"
Who's never fed your drive to find your feet.
Your dada's crushed your cheek; your Christmas treat's
A lessoned brain from manly whacks of ham.
Today his "passive fist" will praise The Lamb
Then hide from gossip's congregation bleat.

Our God is love. I'll save you. If I can.
Your eyes are drugged but desperate for the truth,
No tablet masks the hunger of your heart.
Your growing pain is father to the man
I hold. In life's uncertain lodging, youth
Is crucified by elders from the start.

4. Disco Inferno (Bryn)

I'm Rolling Stoned. I don't know where we are.
A Newport "*Ou se trouve...*" on hands and knees.
I taste her furnace lips and hair and – freeze
And, like a virgin, spooked, I seek the bar.
I try to find myself by forging star
Through streets of foreign syntax to alleys
Blind. Panic "what point in the galaxies
Still? whirled wastes of space! a spin gone too far..."

She finds my wide eyes in the underpass
Not finding themselves. "I like you, why'd you leave?"
I hiss, "Are you Madonna?" and she laughs,
Then holds me as this town's unuttered scream
Yawns empty as The Pit – and I BELIEVE
Her candle in the blue, her milky dream.

5. Blasted (Bron)

He's so mixed up. I'm not sure even I
Am not some mistleberry mother trip
Just holding him together like a zip
Of heavy metal rock – whose force won't die
While I'm content to fasten up his fly
And rock him gently on my rolling hip
And blow his mind and nose but never strip
His docks prescription. Just a valley guy.

But when his prayer is crushed between our lips
And kisses come inside me like a bee's
And draw my honey from me, every drop,
A stillness comes upon me as of ships
That tall and stately slide beneath the sea's
Uncharted depths. "Oh God," I whisper, "stop..."

11. Exile (Bryn)

I had to leave her carrying the child
With carboniferous limestone in my head
And heart of Millstone grit as cold and dead
As all the mountain peaks out in The Wild
I stormed across those days and nights, reviled
By everyone, and me the most, but bled
Of any feeling by the chill, and fed
By streams so hard that even *they*'d have smiled.

The comedown was I had to go away
And never see the babe or her again.
For many years, in English towns, I said
I'd made the break, forgotten both of them.
But now I stand and watch a son at play
Across the silted stream I left for dead.

Yellowing Lines
(or The Hitch Hiker)

The boy I was at eighteen
Came to me in the night, and said,
"You have betrayed me..."

You snore by the side of the poem
I scaled the hills for
(Singing names through the mist,

Appalled by echoes),
And in prose without rhythm
Call her "wife",

Delight in nice distinctions
Of colons and semi-colons,
Tense manipulations

Of your subjunctive moods;
Where I wailed for help,
Eyes wide as space,

Raged at Grammar school discourtesies,
My head crammed with stars.

WHAT HAVE YOU DONE TO ME?"

Learned to drive
A thickening skin

Past ten a c c e l e r a t i n g years

Where I took my stand

        Deserted

In the rain.

Llewellyn The Last

A face off the cover
Of *Songs For Swinging Lovers,*
Grin jaunty with woodbine;
Parks the Jag in George St.
To call in at The Office.

I check my Beatle fringe
In his rearview mirror.
I'm eight and three quarters,
And it's starting to show.

He takes an age but throws
In a real leather football
Newport County couldn't buy.
I'm his daughter's Eldest
After all. I'm *The Son.*

He reverses, one-handed,
Lights up with the other,
Has a pile of funny clocks
And a soiled bag of treasure;
Glides like a Godfather
Past a Police Car;
Calls at eight other offices
Reserved for The Family...

I check my Lennon lenses
In his ex-miner's blue glare.
I'm eighteen, red-tinted,
And "going for a student."

He never really settled
Under Wilson's Law,
It took away his edge.
The racecourse has its own law:
Reckless free enterprise,
Shrewd sharp practice.
The Tote was a closed shop,
Tax was a closed shop,
"Laying off" a bet
Was a closed shop...

I check my Wedding Speech
In his hearing aid. He chuckles,
A "want to start again" smile
Dying on his face.

Marked For Life

Your illegible hand, *Sarah Bitcham*,
Cardiff University 1932,
Was being formed before my mother was even born.
I came under it in your angry rust sunset,
Your lipstick and powder applied as explosively
As your blistering pen.

Simple sentences were all we were capable of
You declared in the accusative. And not a word
We recognised as friendly, or ours,
Or even that brimmed, poet-wise,
Of itself, could we use.
You got your red-hot malice into everything.

Sentenced us to the letter of the language.
Only Mr Lawrence – from his solar
Plexus – and Mr Orwell – from his stubborn
Senses – could liberate us, drunkenly, later
From your three years' regime of cold water
And spiritless pages.

You delighted in Literature as some might in torture.
We were forbidden to write, "I liked the poem
We read by Wordsworth." You'd reduce "I liked" to lashes,
Scald three solid bars across "the poem",
Grill a word as emotive and colloquial as "we"
And with arrows and scrawls that stabbed and blushed
Their brand amid the acne
Add, in your slap-round-the-face Standard English,
Red-ant stinging the page: "Simon Lee, the Old Huntsman
By Wordsworth, is an admirable poem."

The twenty second time you repeated that lesson,
Our Fifth Year bulks crammed through the legs
Of our Third Year desks,
I stopped writing altogether, could only parrot
Your shrieked corrections. But you wounded even those;
Usurped "improved" by "enhanced", not because
It was more accurate (it was less) but because
Like that lesson on gerunds you gave every Wednesday

Afternoon, it proved – as it had for forty years -
How much cleverer you were than us,

How much more incisive you were than the "imbeciles"
Who'd introduced O levels
Fifteen years before; how much sharper was
You Standard tongue than the the rest of the Staff's;
The rest of the valley, fanciful critics, pompous
Academics and, indeed, the whole English speaking world

Except your mother
With whom you still (at 62) lived.

Well, mark this.

Norfolk Seen From The Welsh Mountains

Only a Welshman can really appreciate Norfolk.
Norfolk is Wales in reverse.
It points the other way, the cold flat levels of Europe
instead of the soft wet heights of Ireland.
Its mountains are all under the surface,
Its riches above it.
The openness of Norfolk is the absence of Welsh mountains.
You have to have grown up with gradients all around you to
know this.
The big skies are the big open sigh of *non*-valleys,
the freedom from Welsh impediments.
Instead of grey cloud-capped mountains closing you in -
that great North Sea lapping you out.
Instead of a blood-misted history of towering defiance in
defeat,
generations of stubborn invaders placidly seduced.
Instead of the sunset West haunted with legends of greatness
past,
the level sun rising in the East forever new.
Instead of Arthur the sleeping hero-king, Hereward the *Wake*.
Instead of the furious vowels, the clucking deprecatory
consonants.
Welshman rant with glorious indignation
but always give in in the end.
Norfolkians smile sideways and don't argue
but *never* do what they're told either.
Welshmen rhapsodize about the freedom and calm and the
endless horizons.
Norfolkians take it for granted.

Wales In Norfolk

The spring-white hawthorn is summerberry red
On the hedgerow I drive to school by every day,
A hedgerow under a sloping terraced cowfield,
The nearest I'm going to get to Wales
In Norfolk. Water-meadows, really, despite the heron
And the sea half a mile away. It's wild,
Though, wild as Mynydd Maen in its different way,
Arctic winds – and birds – in winter; this deep
Stillness – a stillness you can't quite trust – in summer:
The mountain ash soft as a rose, the spinney
Winter-gnarled in the harvest sunshine,
And the spring-white hawthorn summerberry red.
I have a slice of the moon in my pocket
And the wild red rose of desire.
I would like them to mean something.
I give the first line of this poem to Merlin in a play
About Guinevere and Arthur, feel the surge of pagan magic
In the prickly male hawthorn; the lady elegance
Of the mountain ash, rosaceae claws sheathed
In full berries of bright scarlet blood.
The august cornfield nods, under the blade in an hour,
A lifetime of growth and weather in every ear.
Another school year swings into place as I ply the gears
Along the streamlet they call a river in these parts
(Boudicca's *Cymru*), spreading a word I know only by heart
– Excalibur, Logres, the myths and spells of Britain -
To young Angles hiding a wild Celtic fringe
Under their stacks of straight yellow hair.
In permanent exile from *Y Gymraeg*,
A tongue as remote to me now as dragons,
It's too late to do anything more
Than write Welsh poetry in translation;
And I'm too far from legend to make a stand
On any more lofty and heroic ground
Than a classroom teaching what I've mastered
Of a foreign language: English. But I don't want to.
I want the summer to go on forever...

*

When tawny-eyed Merlin and Arthur and Guinevere
Return to reclaim the whole of Britain,
And the spring hawthorn and the summer mountain ash
And the pagan-solstice mistletoe of Morgan Le Fay
All bloom together on the same tree,
Maybe then the long exile of the Bards will be over
And I won't have to go to school anymore.

Ofsted

I am being Inspected.
After years of imagining
Little blue-eyed men from Saturn,
they're here!

The one watching me take a register
-noting my hesitation on his clipboard-
looks exactly like Inspector Cluseau.
I feel exactly like Herbert Lom.
He apologises for his trench mac
and tells me he's from Cheshire.
I smile and squeak
o that's nice.
(Chehire my arse!)

The English Inspector
takes 2 days to land.
by which time I am climbing the walls,
leaping out of my skin every time the door opens,
YELLING at kids for talking
during discussion.

Now *she's* here.
The first day in a purple power suit, the second in puce.
When she talks to me, I can't concentrate.
I am fixated on how flat the end of her nose is,
the flat empty plains on the far side of Saturn,
a planet that invented SATS and the National Curriculum.
She might not look like
a little blue-eyed Saturnalian
but underneath that approximation
to a human form
lurks a Blimp & Boffin... Government... Education... Policy.

Wesley *won't* shut up of course.
He never shuts up.
I thought this week of all weeks
that just for once
he would shut up.
I hear myself pleading, wheedling, whingeing,
wielding all the power of fifteen years
teaching syntax, nuance and tone,
"Wes. Wes! there's a bloody Inspector in the room!!
Please PLEASE! PLEASE!! PLEASE!!!!!

SHUT UP!!!!!

The Road To Walsingham

we arrive from wells next the sea
where an old biddy in the sue ryder shop
tried to sell me secondhand knee-length
gentlemen's underpants for twenty manic minutes
no matter how emphatically I refused,
conceding in the end that they weren't perhaps
the type quite in fashion now;
other gems included the battleaxe
in the bookshop grinding her lifetime of grudges
into my back after I'd browsed a Beatles book
for ten seconds without paying; and the ladies
in the Edwardian tea emporium who not only tried twice
to serve us a lasagne we had ordered on neither occasion
but also reacted to Jackie's innocent and rather flattering
request for the recipe for the toffee-apple pecan pie
as if we intended to drive them all into bankruptcy
with a rival toffee-apple pecan pie business next door...
and so to Walsingham, "England's Nazareth",
where, the guide book tells us, "Richeldis de Faverches,
the Lady of the Manor, had visions of Our Lady
in 1061, and obeyed the Virgin's command
to build a replica of the Holy House."
I observe the consequences of this divine town planning:
the fly-pilgrims round the sticky trivia-shops
peddling pardons blessed by St. Margaret (of Grantham)
useless even for the material world, strange fare indeed
for a journey to God; I tap the Valentine's card
I bought elsewhere, secret as the thousand
year longing in my heart-pocket, and feel like a tourist
securing his wallet in a den of thieves.
the barrels of holy water on draught at the shrine
proclaim a Catholic vision "administered by Anglicans":
corndolly Maries and convoluted Angels
fastened with celestial barbed wire and the Queen of Heaven
hoisted aloft like a Guy Fawkes, all completely cuckoo: no
Catholic
like a High Anglican licenced to waft incense

and roll out the jiggery popery; each chapelstall of candles
a wholesale warehouse of birthday-cake wishes:
I think of boxes of shoes, their thousands of soles
worn thin on gas pedals, mundanely going nowhere.
if Richeldis's original vision could somehow
be tested, how many of these ardent pilgrims
would actually care? and if it was true, once,
is this Chinese whisper through ever more
reductionist Ages any God at all by the time
it's been dissolved, evicted, bartered,
claimed and counter-claimed by Catholics, Anglicans,
Methodists, Russian Orthodoxies, junkshops, junkies...?

a holy half mile from that Bank Holiday Sabbath
past a pilgrim or two on foot, is the "Slipper Chapel"
– "the last wayside church for pilgrims
before they came barefoot down into Walsingham.
built in 1325, it is now the Roman Catholic National Shrine
to Our Lady": the chalky green valley slopes
off into heaven. I trace the gentle contours,
the lit, ascetic ash of winter Norfolk,
then light on the flooded stream, water of life
running over in an instant of absolute freedom;
the landscape turns to vision, lightning-flash clear,
fully Earthed, sheep bleating like the bellows of heaven,
the pleasant purl of water on water...

✳

unlatching the heavy, mediaeval door, I catch
the melting warmth of Catholic candles,
Virgin-Motherly; genuflect with the ease of a mason
who knows God's handshake, pray a private prayer
translated from the Ineffable, cross myself out:
the language of the heart
as simple and pure as that painted bird
depicting the holy spirit on the wall above the altar.

then people come in and, with them, rules:
is this the right slot for the coin? is its bellclang
an assault on the Silence? should I touch
that taper or leave the firing of my prayer
to consecrated hands? my daughter slots her fifteen
pence candlemoney into the doffed hat of a pilgrim
by mistake. I gesture, chortling, for its return.
– was that sacrilege? that lady standing in bowed
severity like a Raphael Angel in the shadows,
eyes fixed on the holy spirit, what is she forbidding?
this free wild air I bring in from outside?
this joke Craig yelled from the car still ringing
its half-brick Belfast Paisley in my ear *("Why have ye a bicycle*
under your arm, Ian?" "Sure, I'm holding a rally, son!")?
or is she forbidding the fact that I'm a not-Catholic
in the same way I'm a not-Welshman (Welsh but human too,
Catholic but a Soul beyond religion)? her rules
don't hold the Real me and I need a more absolute way
to assert my Self in the world than these repelling
opposites of the ego, but ego-denial has to start somewhere,
needs an ego to deny, I guess. I leave awkwardly,
balked somehow. the scent of Freedom, that trail of Self
is as strong going out as it was coming in.

Coalminer
MCMLXXXIV

Soiled, solid, solitary figure
Working the thin seam of charity
In the main street.

"TRINDER'S ARE SCAB'S"
In red capitals on the disused railway bridge.
Again by the steps up to Tesco's.

I remember you across ten years,
Bar bulging with butties,
Vanguard of the Revolution.

I was a minor then,
Slim student of history,
Sucking the froth of your strike fund.

Now the young push past,
Jobless, to pay a pound more at Style's
For a record they wouldn't look at in Woolworth's.

And the chronically old,
Their health a non profit-making business,
Pass by with a lean look.

And the Griffithstown *crachach*[6],
The New Inn yuppy:
These are The Crowd now.

I push an old fiver
Into your box.

Futility.

[6] parvenus

The North Sea

I am the sea
and its deep sullen anger
is my anger
and its grey endless spaces
are my spaces
and its icy depths
are mine

I am the coast
and its sticky glitter
its sludge and seawrack
its holiday oasis of bright blue and yellow
its seagulls and shallows
are mine

O but
I am the sea
and its monstrous swell
its elephant surges
its charge and retreat
are mine

I am the sea
and its blind destruction
its timless sculptures
are in my gift
and its welling compassion
is mine

I am the sea
and its rocks and rivers
its wrecks and reelings
its sharks and cockles
are mine

I am the whale
that's devouring the world
I am the gull
with wings of icecap
I am the nimbus
dissolving in thunder

I am cold as death
and quick as the morning
blind as surf
sharp-eyed as salt
I am Neptune and Necros
driftwood and bedrock

I am every drop
on its boundless adventure
across Illusion
I am the sea
and my jeweled infinities
are in each ripple
and my boundless whims
are in each droplet
and my fathomless urges
are in your blood.

Sister

You breathed out a sigh of temporary relief
On a still May evening away from the wreck
Of your heart, your marriage, the life you'd assumed,
Laughing, "*This* is me – in jeans, out of make-up,
Stealing a walk up The Mountain to chat."

It was homely hearing the fine Welsh lilt
Of the girl I'd chanced to grow up with
Naming this incline in Norfolk 'The Mountain'
And knowing that, though you'd have to go back
To your own rocky ground, we had finally met.

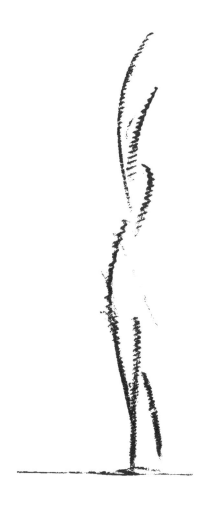

III

The Way of Love
is a Tightrope

i. Sonnets From Hell
ii. Ghazals

A ghazal (pronounced guzzle) is a highly compressed Indian love poem originating in Persia, properly written in Urdu in formally prescribed metrical patterns and rhymed AA BA CA DA etc. It describes states of ecstatic love – and the pain of longing which goes with them – in language that is rhapsodic and thrilling to a degree which seems bizarre in modern English but which once provided the model for the nearest Western equivalent: the Renaissance sonnet (which, like the ghazal, was written to be sung). Even between these two intensely lyrical forms, there is a gap: the gap between East and West. This is marked by the exotic Persian language (e.g. the stock imagery of the nightingale singing to the rose), the blurring of the divide between romantic and mystical and by the form itself which requires that each couplet, while linked by rhyme and metre to the others, stands alone (the sonnet is much more linear and progressive, each section contributing to a whole which is greater than the sum of its parts). These present "ghazals" cannot be classed as such in the classical sense – they are written in English for a start – and the metres adopted are sometimes English ones, sometimes adaptations of Urdu ones and (in two cases) so loose they hardly bear scansion at all. But they do deploy rhapsodic content and language with highly disciplined form (a "synthesis of heart and mind forces"); they concede the importance of the formal rhythms and rhymes in sustaining the emotional tension; they adopt the essential subject (love) and – to a lesser extent – they record an effort to create detachable couplets. In the end, though, the subject has been allowed to drive the poem and if there is some latitude with the rules, this was considered preferable to writing a mere exercise in imitation Urdu.

For further information, see *Coming Home* pages 58-60.

Sonnets From Hell
Both ghazal and sonnet aim heavenwards and at a Beloved (and complain as often as they exult). One's skill in both might be measured as much by one's capacity to love as to write poetry. But while ghazals work with eternal symbols – the rose, the nightingale, the pearl, the cup, wine etc – and can't come down to Earth without losing their spell-like cadence, sonnets seem able to do so much more naturally. (Witness Shakepeare's "My Mistress's Eyes Are Nothing Like the Sun" – or Dante's divine sonnets for the *mortal* Beatrice.) This excerpt from "Sonnets From Hell" traces a failed pilgrimage to India in search of the Eternal Beloved. These sonnets gradually rhyme and then modulate into ghazals.

The last poem of all is neither sonnet nor ghazal in form though it embraces the spirit of both. Typically, being nothing like a ghazal in form, Indians seem to think it is the best ghazal I've written.

I You are Not.

To begin at the beginning: you are not
– Some gracious lady with golden hair,
Whose beauty I could trace, or dress, or undress;
– Single: I went half way round the world
To find another poet kneeling in my place
And there are thousands before and behind;
– *Alive*, let alone here and now with me:
You are not even susceptible to words

And yet I call you and am struggling still
Tongue-tied to please you and to make some sense,
Sure though now I'm not one of your chosen
No matter how infinite your forbearance
Because I speak to the crowd in my heart
Never to the One, the heart itself beating.

II Ocean of Love

So it's difficult to call you *Beloved*
And mean it. And *that's* easy compared
To living it. Nothing to beat a good song,
Though, where the dust and dirt of the gutter
Drain to the love-ocean of the heart
And if I could raise one *genuine* salt tear
I would: your Lovers cry You sea-tales but
Love without salt is not love. It's just wet.

And what can I give you that isn't yours?
Only impossible things. Equipoise
Forbearance, freedom from worry,
Selfless service, cheerfulness! God, I'm so full
Of the opposites of these. Isn't there
Something easier? something I can *do?*

V Nothing Like The Sun

My Master's eyes are brighter than the sun.
Don't *almost* make the day begin, *do*.
Still I know what Shakespeare (and Rex
Harrison) mean: you can't feel absolutes,
Nor make sonnets out of them, only credoes.
Humans cannot bear much Reality:
And to see Sun face to face, or claim to,
Merely deprives us of the squinted stars -

Like *His eyes twinkle at some holy joke*
That He bears the punch of: He swans ahead
Of the in-crowd and knows where He's going:
He is God in Persian form, a tiger's
Grace, a lion's heart. He is the woman
I long for. He is the man I could be.

IX Fever

To have lived once in India is to be
Conscious of the fever behind the plan,
Conscious of the terror behind the calm,
Conscious of darkness in lit Western cities;
So I've flown out again to your lost century
Disbelieving in switch and tap and fan,
An hygenic jet-propelled Western Man,
Disorientated[7] by your love of me.

Now an Asian flu is taking me places
Which have no painless position to lie.
I escape to my mind but it won't stop
Pitching me backwards through haggling faces,
Eyes and voices, my head in a sweat shop,
Your whole suffering country in my heart's sty.

[7] Orientated means literally, turned to the East.

Ocean Eyes

And when you gave, then turned away, your ocean eyes, I knew
My heart would break in waves there on the rocks of losing you.

I didn't ask for this; I only breathed without belief
Unconscious idle prayers: I never dreamed you'd make them true.

My life's in ruins now; I can't go home, nor to your door:
In bars and crowds and churches, all I taste is missing you.

I talk about you all the time and think I've made some sense
But if my words can't bring you near...what good can they do?

My days were full of waiting for your sure feet at my door.
They're empty now your hand has waved you're never coming through.

You touched me once; I closed my eyes; your warmth was like a fire;
I let it smoulder gently: now it blasts my heart in two.

O lover, don't complain, "What can't be lost is never found."
He answers only helpless cries, this angel from the blue.

Angel

The girl I love is an angel, her golden wrist like a rose,
Her body held in a soft flame of stillness, freed in a pose.

The girl I love is an angel, unfastened hair like a tide,
Her fingers fly out of time's rut: and touch my heart as it
blows.

The girl I love is an angel, her mouth a kiss that won't stop;
Her ears in whispering curls hear what open lovers propose.

The girl I love is an angel, her neck is softer than sky;
She turns to me like a planet and everything else explodes.

O bard, this love is a rare draught, you're lost and that's why
you win,
You're stripped of even your held breath, and kiss what God
alone knows.

This one got me to the televised finals of a national ghazal competition in 1992, the only Welsh face in an otherwise comely Asian crowd.

Roses' Thorns

Those who say that marriage is safe, they ought to marry you:
A dozen years of roses' thorns, and still no getting through.

I talk as if I know the score, can sing the words, but still
I love you far too much for me, not near enough for you.

I flirted with your daring once, and called your beauty mine,
Unwarned then of a charge so high, so wild, so overdue.

It takes so long to cleave together, marry all to one,
And if I kiss-you-quick goodbye, I cleave myself in two.

Since love is war, a heart attack, between the good and bad,
I'd offer to surrender: but I'm fighting me not you.

O lover, say it's safe to wed, don't boast your loving's wounds:
The Rose'll think you're ready – that'll be the end of you.

Slices of Infinity

O love! I offer my patience, persistent, brave to the end;
This fickle loving so stiff-scared of life and death, I'll amend.

I'll hold your course through the quicksand, the place to learn to accept
The shifting world as it needs must; accept its ways cannot mend.

I'll cry our love from the rooftops, embrace the hate of the street,
The cold attrition of thick skins, and won't accuse or defend.

I'll fly the rose of this love-truth you've gentled deep in my heart
And stand alone if I have to, no matter how I'm condemned.

Tomorrow's worse if you worry; the past can never be changed:
Would gnaw my mind and my heart sick with wanting both as my friend.

A fretful mind's like a buzzsaw, it hacks the joy from our lives;
But such a kick as I LET GO, it blasts me through to an end.

The Way of Love is a tightrope, it's pitched above the mundane – This circus whirl of allurements his mind is poised to transcend.

O Traveller on unsure ground, your Guide will walk, though you'd run;
It's hard as flint to give True Love and, rushed, you'll only pretend.

This ghazal is closely based on "Some Divine Qualities", a prose discourse by Avatar Meher Baba.

Bak Sheesh

"A pearl beyond the shell of existence and time... my heart sought." *Hafiz.*

I catch your eye out of space-time, a breathless poise out of mind;
A jewel I lost and have long sought, but never dreamed I could find.

I dance with you in my mind's Eye, and pour a rose for your mouth,
And sip your kiss at a drunk's bar where vision comes to the blind.

My heart is clear but my head's fogged, I'm lost in love without trace:
I can't make sense of your bright Smile, the bill you leave me to sign.

I thought your spirit was bak sheesh, I guzzled all of it down.
Next time you're feeling so generous, don't cast your jewels before swine!

My restless deserts of longing create mirages of joy
Which leave the lips of my soul dry and deserts trapped in my mind.

This Love that draws me is so True, I lose my grip on the false;
It calls my heart from a jungle where lovers hunt but don't find.

This Love that draws me is so True, my heart is aching to steal
A pearl for You from my life's shell, a nightingale from the wind.

O pilgrim, longing takes so long and loving's like any ache:
Oblivion is the one cure; His drops of spirit remind.

Bak sheesh: alms for beggars in India. I heard it when I was growing up as working class slang for a "freebie." The word was probably brought home by soldiers of the British Empire.

Beloved, To Please You

Baba, what can I say to please You?
What tuneless song could I try to sing?
What note can I strive for to reach You?
In Your Presence words fail and are nothing.

Baba, what can I do to keep You?
Close to my heart as it beats out my time?
Close in the crowds where I speak with You?
In Your Presence words fail and are nothing.

Baba, what can I think of to praise You?
If I mastered expression in everything?
If I measured Your Grace in a poem for You?
In Your Presence words fail and are nothing.

Baba, what deepest bow could raise You?
Were the depths of humility sounded?
Were my debt to You found and expounded for You?
In Your Presence words fail and are nothing.

Baba, what heights of beauty could touch You?
Could the world rest in laurels at my feet?
Could I sing like Orpheus in the deep for You?
In Your Presence words fail and are nothing.

Baba, what kind of love could I utter You?
Would my heart were an Ocean pouring?
Would my life were an answer to Your calling for You?
In Your Presence words fail and are nothing.

Baba, what can I know to impress You?
Should all of my moments come clear?
Should all my inspirations come together for You?
In Your Presence words fail and are nothing.

Baba, what kind of sense can I make for You?
Can I open my heart and reveal it ALL?
Can I seek to know Your Word and express it for You?
In Your Presence words fail and are nothing.

Beloved, these questions I ask of You,
Yet Love asks no questions, and answers none.
I am lost, but in love I am lost in You.
In Your Presence my failings mean nothing.